ANIMALS IN THE QURAN

PROPHET YUNUS (A) & THE WHALE

AL-KISA
FOUNDATION
WWW.KISAKIDS.ORG

KISA KIDS
PUBLICATIONS

Prophet Yunus (a) lived in the beautiful green land of Nainawa. Most people in Nainawa were farmers, and Allah gave them many blessings, like beautiful green hills and delicious fruits. But instead of thanking Allah, most of them refused to believe in Allah.

Prophet Yunus (a) tried to guide the people and teach them about Allah. They all loved him because he was so kind, but they still didn't believe in Allah.

Prophet Yunus (a) tried guiding them for many, many years! But after so many years, only a few people began to believe in Allah. The rest were stubborn! No matter how many signs Prophet Yunus (a) showed them, they still did not believe!

Prophet Yunus (a) didn't know what else he could do! So, He prayed to Allah to solve this problem. Allah answered him and said that He would send a great punishment soon.

The next day, Prophet Yunus (a) went to his people and warned them about the punishment that was coming soon! However, the people still didn't listen to him, and Prophet Yunus (a) became sad.

There was barely any time left! The punishment was almost here! It was too hard for Prophet Yunus (a) to be around his people. They could see all the signs of the punishment, but they still weren't asking for forgiveness! So, he left as soon as he could. He went towards the sea and boarded a boat that sailed him far into the ocean.

Finally, it was time for the punishment! When the people of Nainawa saw the storm coming, they became very afraid! One man suggested, "Let's go towards the mountains and ask Allah to forgive us! Maybe He will remove His punishment!"

Every single person, from the young to the old, began crying. Finally, for the first time after so many years, they prayed to Allah!

The people of Nainawa put their trust in Allah for the first time and asked Him for forgiveness. Allah is the Most Kind! So, of course, He immediately forgave them and sent away the punishment! Alhamdulillah! Everyone thanked Allah and promised to follow Him and His Prophet from now on!

Meanwhile, a large, hungry whale approached Prophet Yunus' (a) boat. It wouldn't leave until it could eat one of the passengers. "What should we do?!" one of the passengers asked, "How do we decide who to throw overboard?"

"Let's pick names from a hat! That's most fair," another passenger suggested, and they all agreed. They picked a name from the hat three times, and Prophet Yunus' (a) name came out each time!

Prophet Yunus (a) trusted Allah and knew this was what He wanted. So, he calmly jumped into the ocean and let the whale swallow him in one gulp.

Allah told the whale not to hurt Prophet Yunus (a). Prophet Yunus (a) thanked Allah and thought, *Now I can worship Allah somewhere no one else has!* As he sat in the whale's dark stomach, Prophet Yunus (a) recited tasbeeh and prayed to Allah. Over time, his powerful prayers lit up the whale's entire stomach with blessings!

A few days later, the whale finally spat out Prophet Yunus (a)! Because he hadn't eaten in so many days, he was very weak! So, Allah made a squash plant grow next to him on the shore. The plant protected him from the sun, kept away the insects, and gave him plenty of fruit so he could become strong again!

The tribe of Nainawa was thrilled to hear that Prophet Yunus (a) was still alive! As he walked back into town, they all gathered to greet and hug him. They couldn't wait for him to teach them all about Allah!

Prophet Yunus (a) lived for a long, long time! The people spent every moment they could with him learning about Allah! *Alhamdulillah*, they had finally accepted the truth! In return, Allah rewarded them with many more blessings!

From the people of Nainawa, we see how it's never too late to turn to Allah! Allah is the Most Powerful, and only He can save us, even from the belly of the whale!